違警罪図解 : 刑法抄出

Focus on Criminal Law:
An Illustrated Guide to Misdemeanor Crimes

or

Rules for Living in Nagoya

Published 1881

Edited and Illustrated by:

今江五郎 Imae Goro

Translated by Eric Shahan

Cover Image:

A True View of Nagoya, Bishu Domain 尾州名古屋真景
100 Famous Views from All Over the Country 諸国名所百景
By Utagawa Hiroshige

Translator's Introduction

Overview

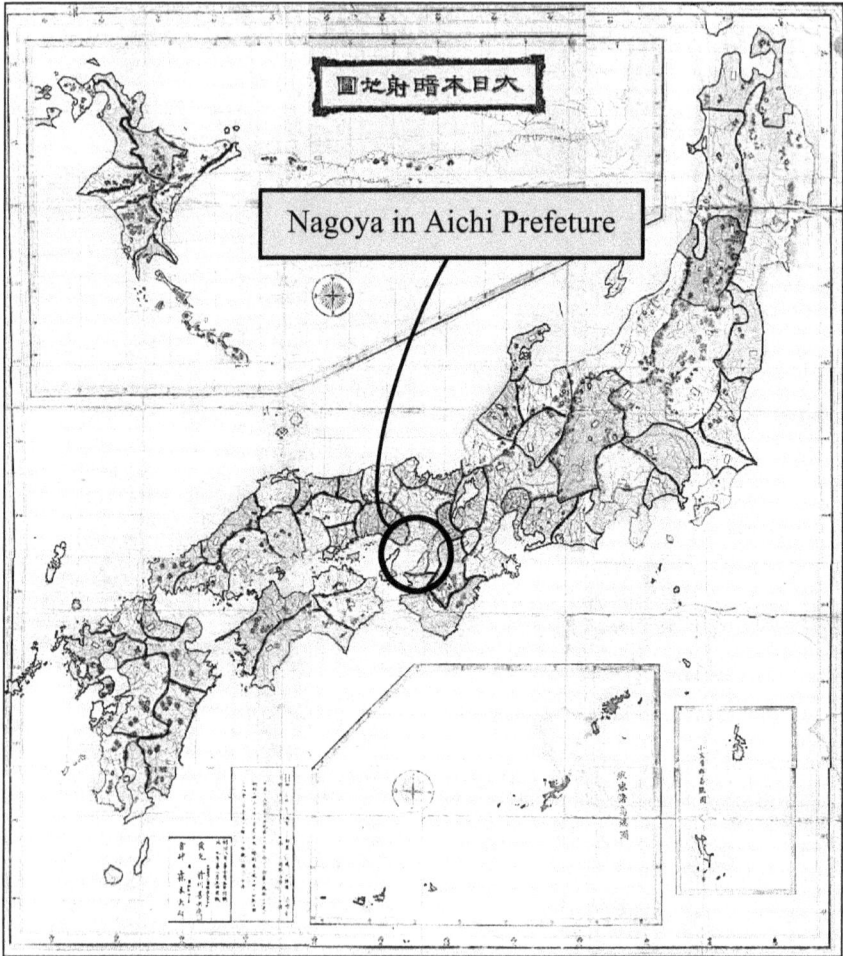

Map of Japan from the 8th year of the Meiji Emperor (1875).

The Meiji Restoration in 1868 ended the nearly 300-year control of the government by the Tokugawa Shogunate. The new Meiji government completely reshaped Japan and made sweeping changes to how everyday citizens lived their lives.

Reorganization of the Whole Country

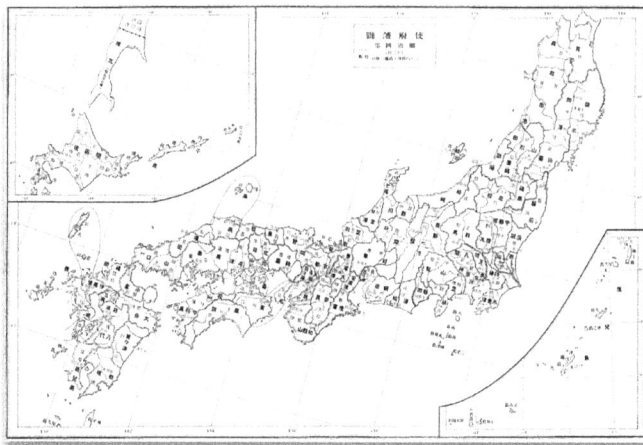

An 1872 map showing the 72 prefectures

Up until 1868 Japan was divided into Han, or Domains, each ruled by a Daimyo, feudal lord, that collected taxes and had their own army. In 1871 the government decided to implement *Haihan-chiken* 廃藩置県, or the scrapping of the feudal domain system in favor of a reduced number of prefectures. The Daimyo, who headed each domain, had to return their authority to the Meiji Emperor. In exchange, they were left in control of their former domains, albeit as non-hereditary governors.

Initially, the feudal domains were converted to 305 prefectures. They were gradually reduced as follows:

1871 – 75 Prefectures
1872 – 72 Prefectures
1873 – 63 Prefectures
1875 – 62 Prefectures
1876 – 38 Prefectures

However, after the 1876 decision there was a lot of grumbling about how some prefectures were extremely large, with corresponding questions about how to manage such a large area. Therefore in 1889 the number was increased to 45 prefectures, with Okinawa being added in 1879 and Hokkaido in 1886.

Social Classes

Edo Era illustration showing the four classes in Japan.

The social hierarchy changed as Japan abolished the feudal system with the Meiji Restoration. During the Edo Era (1600~1867) the class system was known as Shi-No-Ko-Sho 士農工商, or four divisions of society. Society was divided as follows:

Shi– The Samurai (around 10% of the population) were the rulers, superior in both their status and the example they set.
No – The farmers (over 80% of the population) were second because they produced the food necessary for society.
Ko – The craftsmen and artisans (around 5%) were placed next since they made things for people to use.
Sho – Merchants (around 5%) were ranked the lowest since they sold things made by others.

In addition, 1% of the population was in the priesthood and another 1% were considered outcasts. However, with the Meiji Restoration in 1868, Japanese could change their social class, where they lived and their occupation.

Abolishing the Katana

Beginning in 1869 laws were being debated regarding eliminating the wearing of Katana. Should the new government abolish the wearing of the long and short Katana, the symbol of Samurai rank? The law was controversial with proponents arguing that new, modern Japan should, "Move away from barbaric practices." While those in favor of maintaining the tradition argued that, "Abandoning wearing the Katana will erode fighting spirt and degrade the vitality of our Imperial Country."

Eventually the government decided on the former course of action and the *Sword Abolishment Edict* 廃刀令 was issued in March of 1876. It prohibited carrying swords in public, with the exception of former Daimyo, the military and police. Violators would have their Katana confiscated. The illustration above, from the April 4th 1876 edition of the *Tokyo Illustrated Newspaper* shows a constable confronting a travelling ex-Samurai, who is still wearing a long and short sword. The Meiji government concluded that, "Since a police force had been established, wearing a sword for self-defense is no longer necessary."

Removing the Samurai's Topknot

The Meiji Emperor in 1873

Zangiri hairstyle

Since ancient times men and women in Japan have had long hair, either tied up in some fashion or allowed to hang down. Traditionally, to cut your hair short was an indication of a separation from society, repentance, or punishment. Danpatsu, or shaving the head, was something done before setting out as a travelling monk or indicative of official punishment. Even today when Sumo wrestlers retire, they hold a ceremony to remove the Chonmage topknot, signifying their retirement.

In Meiji 4 (1871) a *Sanpatsu Datto Rei* was issued by the government. This meant that for official meetings between the Japanese governments and representatives of other nations they would have their hair "free," as in not tied in a Chonmage, in addition to not wearing a sword. Further, dignitaries from other nations would be received in a room prepared with, "chairs with high legs" and a "table." Everyone would also receive guests while wearing shoes.

This rule only applied to government officials, and the general populous was both quite attached to the Chonmage style and resistant to the Sanpatsu, "free hair" style. However, in 1873 the Meiji Emperor had his picture taken with his hair in a Western style. This led to a boom in Zangiri and other Western style haircuts.

The reasoning behind these changes was the Meiji governments desire to rapidly become "modern" and civilized." Foreigners had often commented that the Chonmage hairstyle was representative of Japan's undeveloped culture, thus the Meiji government sought to abandon this old practice.

Police and Criminal Law

Photograph from the late 19ᵗʰ re-creating how criminals were transported after being arrested.

Earliest Police in Japan

The earliest example of policing can be found in the Kojiki, written in the 8th century.

In the age of the gods, Ninigi-no-Mikoto瓊瓊杵尊,the grandson of the sun goddess Amaterasu and the great-grandfather of Japan's first emperor, descended from Heaven. He brought rice and order to earth. On his journey to earth he was protected by many deities, including Aatsukume no Mikoto, who was armed with the Stone Quiver on his back, Kobu Sword on his belt, Heavenly Wave bow in his hand, which was nocked with the True Deer Child arrow.

-History Of Aichi Prefecture Police

Edo Era Police

In the Edo Era (1600-1868) the police stations were called Machi Bugyosho and the administer of such a station was the Machi Bugyo, a high ranking Samurai. This Samurai acted as the Chief of Police as well as the chief prosecutor and judge. There were around 16 of these officials spread out over Japan and Edo city had two, North Station and South Station.

Next in rank under the Machi Bugyo were the Yoriki, who were lower ranked Samurai constables. Each police station in Edo had 25 Yoriki. Under the Yoriki were Doshin, Patrol Officers. The Doshin were also Samurai, however they were of a lower rank. They patrolled the streets, conducted investigations, and also served as prison guards, which meant they assisted with executions. They had the most direct contact with the Chonin, "city folk." There were a hundred Doshin assigned to each police station in Edo. The population of Edo around that time was around 500,000 city folk, with the total for all the area covered by Edo city being a million people.

With so few official police patrolling the streets, the Doshin employed Okappiki 岡っ引, Informant-assistants. The Okappiki were typically former criminals, who were given leniency in exchange for working as assistants and informants. The Okappiki were non-Samurai so they were not permitted to carry lethal weapons, though most carried a "pocketknife" as well as rope and a Jutte truncheon. Their official name was Goyokiki 御用聞き "Official Listeners" however they were called different things in different regions. The Okappiki name was actually quite derogatory as they were former criminals and sometimes resorted to bullying citizens for "protection money." There were around 500 of them in employ.

Meiji Era Police

Under the Tokugawa Government the main purpose of the police department can, in no uncertain terms, be said to have been less about,

Protecting the citizenry and ensuring their enrichment and happiness and more about maintaining the stability of the Tokugawa Bakufu Government.
-Ninety Years of Police Department Martial Arts History
警視庁武道九十年史 1962.

In the early days just after the Meiji Restoration, a system for policing was no longer in place. Soldiers from the various victorious forces that had participated in the Boshin conflict began acting, "Bojaku-bujin 傍若無人, or behaving outrageously." In response to this there were various types of measures enacted that, through a trial-and-error method, ended up with the current Japanese Police system. The following five stages roughly outline how this occurred.

Shichu Torishimari Jidai 市中取締時代
Citywide Control Era

The first method of modern policing the Meiji government tried was called the Citywide Control Era. On February 17th of the 4th year of Keio, 1868 the former Machibugyo, Mr. Ishikawa Toshimura (?-1868) was ordered to take charge of keeping order in the city until the new police system began. Unfortunately, he committed Seppuku on his first day of work and the job fell to a subordinate.

Hanhei Jidai 藩兵時代
The Era of Using Ex-Domain Soldiers

In April of 1868 the government enlisted troops from a total of twelve areas including Kii, Choshu, Satsuma, Bizen and Saga and called the collection Hanhei, or Domain Troops. The Hahei were patrolled in groups to maintain order and protect the citizenry.

Unfortunately, despite having been assigned the important task of maintaining public safety the Hanhei began to dine and drink without paying, threaten people with impunity and, in the worst cases, robbed and stole. Therefore the Hanhei were disbanded.

In November of 1868, still the first year of Meiji, 200 soldiers from Oshi Han were provisionally dispatched to Tokyo as peacekeepers and the method for maintaining the peace began to be reformed.

Fuhei Jidai 府兵時代
The Era of Tokyo Metropolitan Soldiers

In December of 1868 soldiers from thirty domains were selected and brought to Tokyo. They were then reorganized into the Fuhei, or metropolitan soldiers, and assigned to a part of the city. This system spread to other areas of Japan as well and lasted until 1871 whereupon the Ministry of Justice (1871-1948) was founded, and the police were split from the military.

Rasotsu Jidai 邏卒時代
The Patrolling Soldier Era

By 1870, many regions of Japan found that the Fuhei system was lacking and were seeking a more comprehensive solution to policing. The Rasotsu System was established in October of 1871, which was standard uniformed soldiers, who were all trained the same way. While they initially patrolled with swords this was soon abandoned in favor of a standard 90 cm Konbo 棍棒 or club.

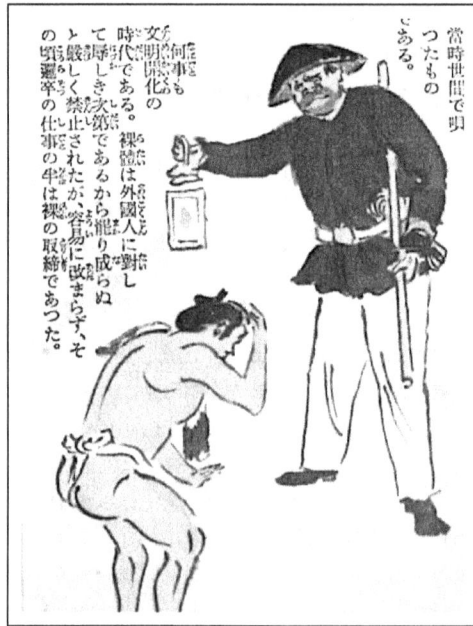

A Rasotsu Patrol Officer wearing the traditional white slacks and carrying a Konbo. He is confronting a man in violation of the 1871 ordinance against being inappropriately dressed.

The ban on wearing a sword for Rasotsu had the unexpected consequence of causing the number of applicants to fall by half. Apparently, the appeal of becoming a Rasotsu was the fact that you could wear a sword. The general consensus was that was that they went from being a Samurai (armed with a sword) to something akin to a prison guard (armed only with a club).

Junsa Jidai 巡査時代
Era of the Patrol Officer

In the 1870's Kawaji Toshiyoshi 川路利良 （1834~1879）travelled to France and returned with an idea of how to model Japan's police department after European and American systems. He later served as the first head of the national police force.

川路 利良 Kawaji Toshiyoshi （1834-1879）

In 1872 the position of Junsa 巡査, or Patrol Officer, was established replacing the Rasotsu. The following are some facts regarding this early type of Japanese police officer.

The Requirements to Become a Junsa Patrol Officer:

- Between the ages of 20-40
- Healthy and over 5 Shaku (165cm) in height
- To agree with the laws of Japan and the Police and have a working knowledge of Japanese History
- To be able to read typical documents and be capable of writing
- A person in control of themselves and able to show restraint

Salary for Junsa Police Officers

- Pay starting at 10 Yen for a First Class Junsa and down to 4 Yen for a Fourth Class Junsa per month.
- Depending on ability and response to crimes pay can increase
- In particular, if a fine is set, half the money will be paid to the officer.
- Further, if an arsonist is stopped an additional 20 Sen will be paid
- If the officer recovers a drowned body an additional 50 Sen will be paid.
- If a robber is caught then 10 Yen will be paid.
- Summer and winter uniform provided and shoe allowance of 3 Yen 50 Sen.

To put the salary in contemporary terms, "1 Yen" was equivalent to about $200. Around this time a schoolteacher made 8 ~ 9 Yen per month with an experienced worker or carpenter around 20 Yen. Thus a Junsa Patrol Officer's salary was fairly low and there was a saying that went, "No one is going to marry a Junsa!" The Junsa, who wore western style clothing, began to be referred to as Omawari San, or *Those That Walk About* by the populace.

Though initially unarmed, in the 7th year of Meiji (1874,) Junsa were again authorized to wear a sword due to anti-government activity. Some of the police were even formed into fighting units and engaged in battle in the Satsuma Rebellion of 1877. Eventually a Taiken Keikan, or Police Officers Armed With Swords, division was created, though members were almost exclusively from former Samurai families, excluding police officers from the general populace.

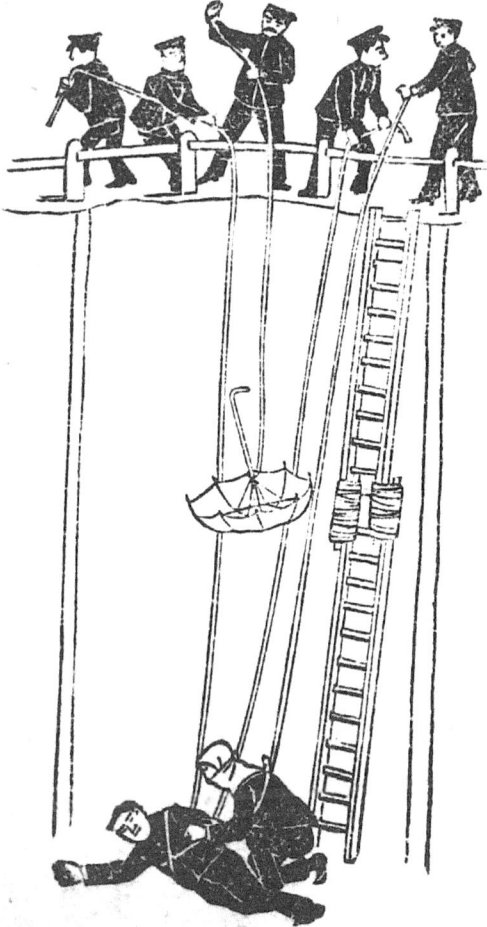

Illustration from a 1915 Japanese rescue guide for police. This shows how to rescue a person who has fallen into an area near poison gas. It advises to use an umbrella for ventilation, and also lowering a candle into the area. If the flame on the candle wavers then there is probably some poisonous gas present.

Reasoning Behind the New Laws

In 1870, the new Meiji government issued a set of laws for minor infractions. These were based on a combination of Japanese law, such as the ones found in *The100 Judicial Decrees* 御定書百箇条 written in 1745, as well as Western and Chinese laws. The Western laws were incorporated into the new Japanese legal system because of the Meiji governments tendency to craft policy with a pro-Western influence. This was termed *Move away from Asia, Accept European Influence* 脱亜入欧.

The goal of the new civil code was to modernize and Westernize Japan's culture. Other terms used to justify the new policies are:

文明開化 *Bunmei Kaikaka*
Civilization and enlightenment. This was a key phrase in Japan's Westernization movement. The phrase could also be translated as "opening up to civilization."

見苦敷風習 *Migurushiki-Fushu*
Describing Early Meiji Era traditions as unsightly and shameful.

卑敷風俗 *Hishiki Fushu/Narifuri*
Like the previous term, this phrase also laments Japan's indecent cultural traditions.

御国体 *Gokokutai*
This phrase refers to the Nation of Japan as a Whole, its image. This term was used to indicate the *Migurushi-Fushu* were adversely affecting the image of Japan on the world stage.

裸体 *Ratai*
Naked bodies. The Japanese tradition of carpenters, rickshaw drivers, porters and steeplejacks of working in just a Fundoshi loincloth, was referred to as "naked." There was an additional source of "nakedness" with the public bath houses. Most Japanese did not have a bath at their house and used public baths. It was quite common for men to walk home from the bath house in only a *Fundoshi* loincloth.

Implementation of the New Laws For Minor Infractions

The central government first crafted 90 regulations in 1872 and in the following year, they were distributed to all the prefectures. These regulations were considered a guideline to be adapted by the local government according to their circumstances. These regulations were enforced by the newly created police force, known as Junsa Patrol Officers. These patrol officers would spot violations and issue punishment or fines on the spot. The regulations were based on how the French police handled minor breaks in the law. It was also influenced by London, Shanghai and Hong Kong police procedures.

A French legal expert named Gustave Émile Boissonade de Fontarabie (1825 –1910) was invited to Japan to assist with crafting Japan's civil code. Boissonade lived in Japan from 1873 to 1895 teaching at the Law School of the Ministry of Justice. He worked with Ume Kenjiro and Hozumi Nobushige on drafting Japan's new criminal and civil code.

These regulations were intended as a stopgap measure and used from 1872 until 1885 when they were replaced by more refined system called Police Violation Crime 違警罪. These laws were divided into 3 categories of infraction, light and severe. The Police Violation Crimes system was kept until 1948 when it was replaced by the Minor Crime Law.

Each area hired printers to make illustrated versions in order for the regulations to be made easily available to the public. This book was edited and illustrated by Imae Goro and published on February 7th of Meiji 14 (1881.) Mr. Imae refers to himself as a "Heimin" or Commoner from Aichi Prefecture. This is opposed to Shizoku, which would mean a person of Samurai heritage. No other information regarding Imae Goro could be found. He also published a book titled *How to Draw Birds and Flowers* 花鳥画式.

Sparrow and Plum Blossoms   *Pheasant and Braken*
From: *How to Draw Birds and Flowers*花鳥画式

Rules for Living in Nagoya

By Imae Goro · Published 1881

刑法抄出　違警罪圖解　全

今江五郎解

第二十六號

刑法別冊ノ通改定候條此旨

布告候事

但實際施行ノ期日ハ追テ布告スヘキ事

明治十三年七月十七日　左大臣熾仁親王

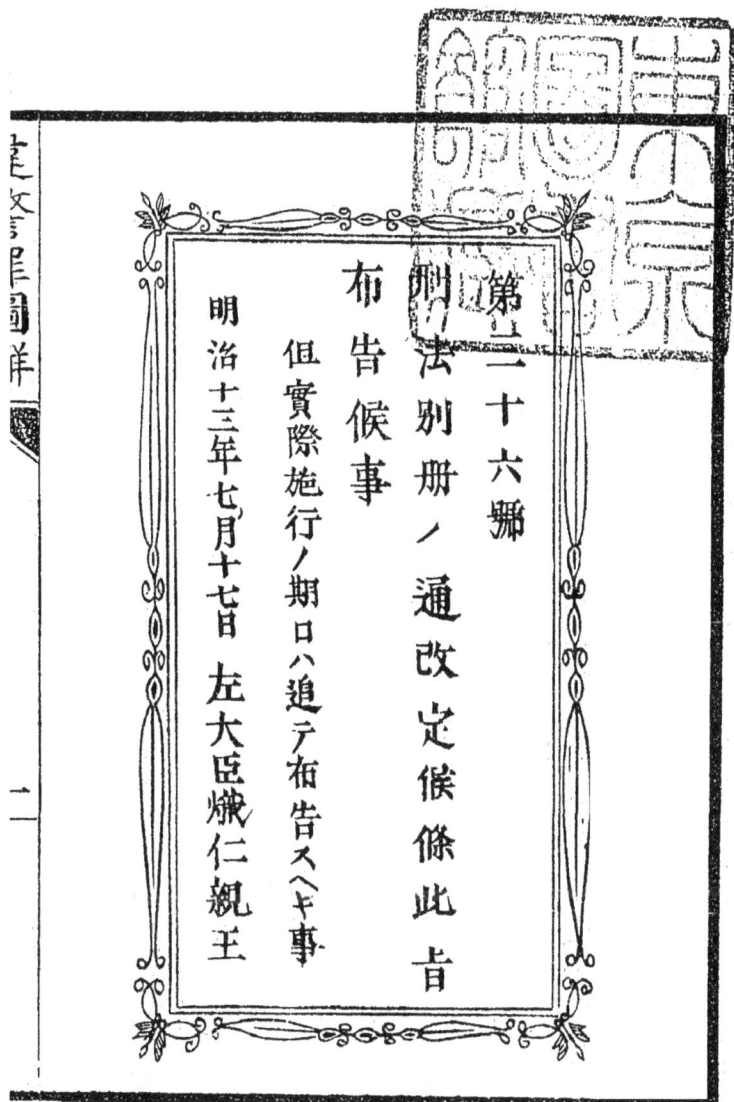

Government Directive 26

This pamphlet announces changes to the legal code.　However, the actual date of implementation will be announced at a later time.

July 7th Meiji 13 (1880)

Arisugawa-no-miya Taruhito-Shinno

有栖川宮熾仁親王 (1835 ～ 1895)

3

Illustration of a Japanese Courthouse

違警罪図解　二一

今江五郎編輯

第四百二十五條　左ノ諸件ヲ犯シタル者ハ三日以上
十日以下ノ拘留ニ處シ又ハ壹圓以上壹圓九十五錢
以下ノ科料ニ處ス

（一）
規則ヲ遵守
セスシテ焔薬
其他破裂スヘキ
物品ヲ市街ニ
運搬シタル者

（二）
規則ヲ遵守
セスシテ火薬其他
破裂ス可キ物品又ハ焔
次ヲ發ス可キ物品ヲ
貯藏シタル者

1. Any person who does not respect the law and carries gunpowder or any material with explosive properties into the city is in violation.

2. Any person who does not respect the law and stores gunpowder, any material with explosive properties or flammable material is in violation.

Regulation 425

Any person who violates the laws described on the following pages will be subject to imprisonment of not less than three days and not more than 10 days. In addition, a fine of not less than 1 yen and not more than 1 yen 95 Sen must be paid.

This book was edited by Imae Goro.

違式詿違条例角

二

5. Anyone who ignores regulations and builds a steam powered machine or construction with a chimney is in violation. This includes repairing or cleaning such contraptions.

3. Any person who makes or sells fireworks without official permission is in violation.

FIREWORKS

4. Playing indiscriminately with fireworks or other flammables in a crowded residential area is a violation.

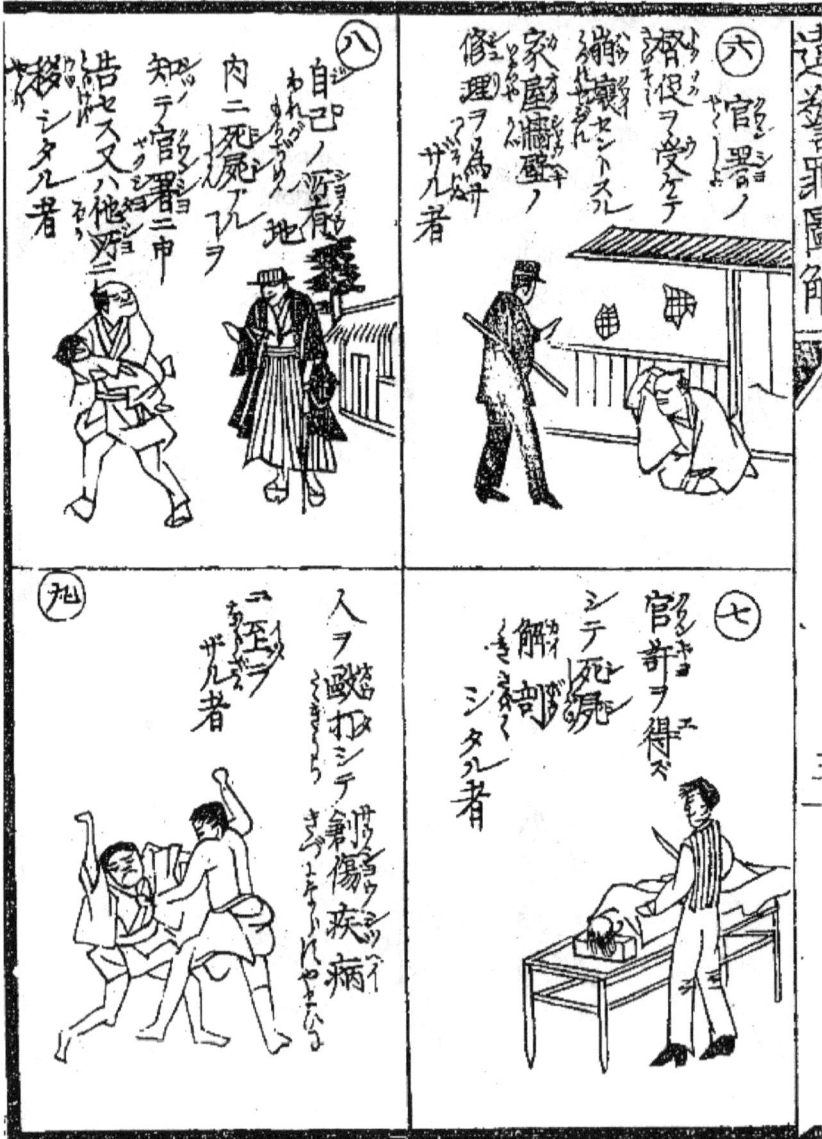

（八）
自己ノ受ケ居ル地
内ニ死屍アルヲ
知テ官署ニ申
告セス又ハ他地ニ
移シタル者

（六）
官署ノ
許沒ヲ受ケテ
隤壊セシ...スル
家屋牆壁ノ
修理ヲ為サ
ザル者

（七）
官許ヲ得ス
シテ死屍ヲ
解剖
シタル者

（九）
人ヲ歐打シテ剌傷疾病
ニ至ラシムルニ至ラ
ザル者

10

8. Any person who fails to report a dead body on their property to the authorities is in violation. This also applies to anyone who moves a dead body to another property.

6. Anyone who has been ordered to perform repairs on a dilapidated house, shop or wall by an official and fails to do so is in violation.

9. Anyone who strikes another person hard enough to cause an injury requiring hospitalization is in violation.

7. Any person who dissects a body without official permission is in violation.

（十）
密ニ賣淫ヲ爲シ又ハ其媒合ヲ爲シ密止ヲ爲シタル者

（十一）
定リタル住居ナク平生營業ノ産業ナクシテ諸方ニ徘徊スル者

（十二）
人ノ住居セザル家屋内ニ潜伏シタル者

（十三）
官許ノ墓地外ニ於テ私ニ埋葬スル者

12. Any person wandering around with no fixed domicile and no fixed occupation or business is in violation.

10. Any person illegally engaged in prostitution or dressing and acting in the manner of a prostitute is in violation.

13. Any person who digs a grave and holds a funeral outside the officially designated area is in violation.

11. It is illegal to sneak into and occupy a house that is not your property.

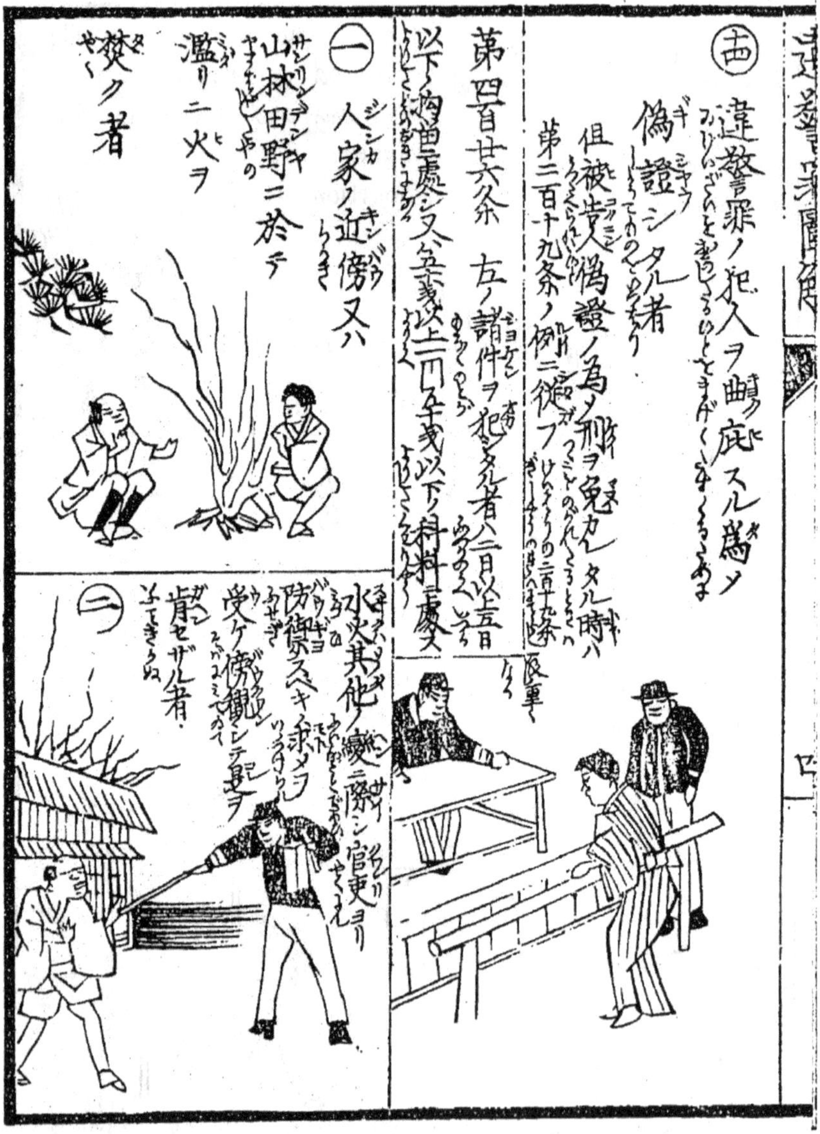

違警罪即決例

（古）

違警罪ノ犯人ヲ蔽庇スル為メ偽證シタル者

但被告人ハ鴻證ノ為ノ那ヲ免カレタル時ハ第三百十九条ノ例ニ循フ

第四百廿六条　左ノ諸件ヲ犯シタル者ハ二月以上四年以下ノ科料處

以下ハ但處ニ又ハ同義ヨリ

一　人家ノ近傍又ハ山林田野ニ於テ濫リニ火ヲ焚ク者

焚ク者や一

二　水火其他ノ變ニ際シ官吏ヨリ防禦スヘキ求メヲ受ケ傍観シテ肯セザル者

14

Regulation 426

Violators of the following regulations will be imprisoned in a facility for not less than 2 days and not more than 5 days. In addition, they will have to pay a fine of not less than 50 Sen and not more than 1 yen 50 Sen.

1. Starting a fire near houses or in the mountains, forests or fields for no clear reason is a violation.

2. Refusing to leave the site of a flood, fire or other disaster despite being ordered to by

an official is a violation.

14.

Anyone who gives false testimony in order to hide the whereabouts of a person guilty of a police regulation offence.
If a punishment will be handed down to the accused, then follow the sentencing examples in regulation 219.

（三）
又ハ腐敗シタル飲食物
不熟ノ菓物
ヲ販賣
シタル者

（四）
健康ヲ保護スル
為メ設ケラレタル
規則又ハ傳染病
豫防規則ニ
違背シタル者

（五）
人ノ通行ス可キ
場所ニアル危撥ノ井溝其他
凹所ニ蓋ス八防圍ヲ
爲サベル者

5. It is a violation to dig a well or any sort of hole and fail cover it with a lid or construct a fence around it.

3. Any person selling unripe fruits is in violation. This also includes selling rotten or poorly prepared food or drink.

4. Any person who ignores the requirements for caring for a person in poor health is in violation. This also includes ignoring official policies regarding communicable disease.

（六）
路上ニ於テ犬
其他禽獸ノ
類ヲ曝シ
又ハ驚逸セシメ
タル者

（八）
在犬拕獸等
繋鎖ヲ怠リ
路上ニ放チ
タル者

（七）
發狂人ノ
看守ヲ怠リ
路上ニ
徘徊セシメ
タル者

（九）
變死人ノ
撿視ヲ
受ケズシテ
埋葬シタル者

五

8. Any owner of a crazy or aggressive dog who fails to secure it with a chain and allows it to roam the streets is in violation.

6. Any person who intentionally startles a dog or any other bird or wild animal is in violation. This includes anyone provoking horses.

9. Any person who buries the body of a person who died under suspicious circumstances without notifying officials is in violation.

7. If a person responsible for the care of a lunatic fails in that duty and allows them to wander about, then they are in violation.

（十）
墓碑及ヒ路上ノ
神仏ヲ毀損シ又ハ汚
瀆シタル者

（十一）
公然人ヲ罵
詈嘲弄シタ
ル者
但訴ヘヲ待テ
其罪ヲ論ズ

違式詿違図解

（十二）
神祠
仏堂其他公ノ
建造物ヲ
汚瀆シタル者

第四百二十七条　右ノ諸件ヲ把シタル
者ハ一日以上三日以下ノ拘留ニ處シ
又ハ二十銭以上一円二十五戔以下ノ
科料ニ處ス

六一

12. It is a violation to insult or ridicule a person in public. However, a decision will not be made until after the incident is reported.

10. It is a violation to damage graves or any statues of gods or the Buddha on the side of the road.

This also applies to anyone who vandalizes them.

Regulation 427

Anyone guilty of the following infractions can be subject to imprisonment of at least 1 day and not more than 3 days and a fine of at least 20 Sen and not more than 1 Yen, 25 Sen.

11. Any person who defaces a Shinto Shrine, Buddhist Temple, any public building or construction is in violation.

違式詿違罪目解

（一）
濫リニ車馬ヲ
疾駆シテ行人ノ
妨害ヲ
為シタル者

（二）
制止ヲ肯ゼズ
シテ人ノ群集
シタル場所ニ
車馬ヲ
牽タル者

（三）
夜中燈火
ナクシテ
車馬ヲ
疾駆スル者

（四）
水石等ヲ
道路ニ堆積シテ
防囲ヲ設ズ
又ハ標識ノ
点燈ヲ怠リタル者

3. Any person pulling a cart or riding a horse rapidly at night without a lantern is in violation.

1. Any person who recklessly pulls a cart or palanquin at high speed, thereby interfering with pedestrians, is in violation.

4. Stacking up lumber or rocks in the road without erecting a safety fence around it is a violation. This also applies to those who do not put a safety lantern out at night.

2. Any person who fails to comply with a "no carts or horses sign" and continues to pull a cart or horse into an area crowded with people.

（七）汚穢物ヲ道路家屋園圃ニ投擲シタル者

（五）瓦礫ヲ道路家屋園圃ニ投擲シタル者

（六）禽獣ノ死屍ヲ道路ニ棄擲シ又ハ取除カサル者

（八）警察ノ規則ニ違背シテ工商ノ業ヲ為シタル者

24

7. Throwing garbage into the road, or near a house, business or someone's garden is a violation.

5. Anyone throwing gravel or broken roof tiles at a house, business or garden alongside the road is in violation.

8. It is a crime to operate a business against police directives.

6. Anyone who disposes of the carcass of a bird or beast in the roadway along with anyone who does not collect such a carcass when directed to do so is in violation.

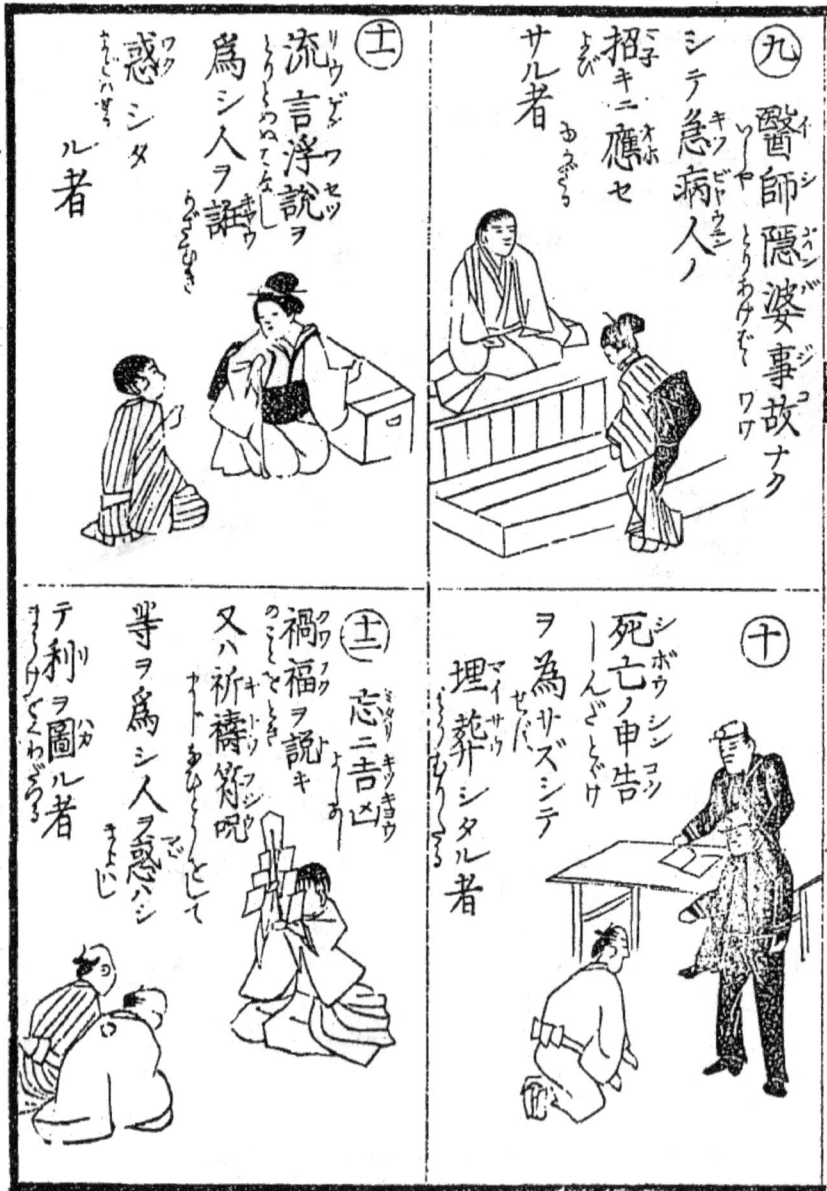

（九）
醫師隱婆事故ナクシテ急病人ノ招キニ應セサル者

（十）
死亡ノ申告ヲ為サズシテ埋葬シタル者

（十一）
流言浮說ヲ為シ人ヲ謗リ惑シタル者

（十二）
禍福ヲ說キ又ハ祈禱符呪等ヲ為シ人ヲ惑ハシテ利ヲ圖ル者

11. Any person who repeats popular rumors with the intention of deceiving or cheating people is in violation.

12. Any person who summons a doctor or midwife under the pretext of a dire emergency when none such emergency exists is in violation.

12. Claiming to be able to interpret good and bad fortune or being in the business of selling good luck charms or talismans for the purpose of deceiving people is in violation.

10. Any person burying a body without filing a report is in violation.

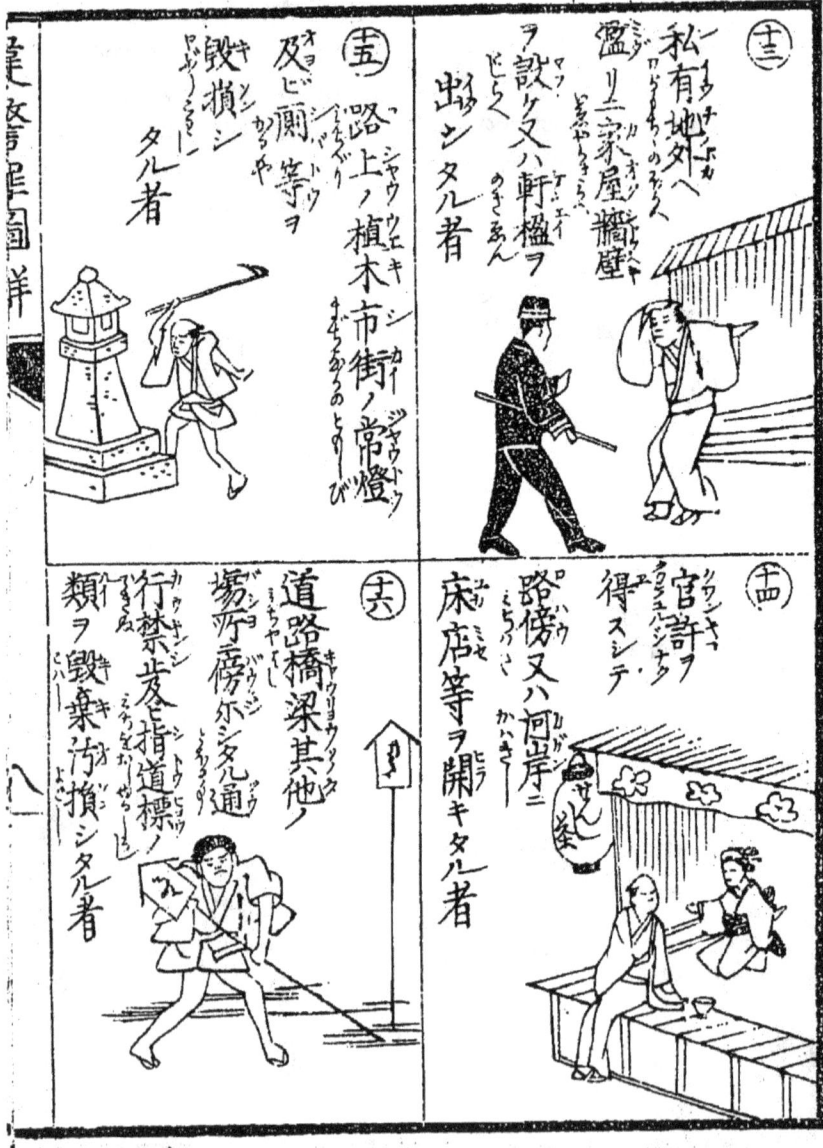

（十三）
一　私有ノ地外ヘ
盗リ家屋橋壁
ヲ設ケ又ハ軒櫺ヲ
出シタル者

（十四）
官許ヲ得スシテ
路傍又ハ河岸ニ
床店等ヲ開キタル者

（十五）
路上ノ槙木市街ノ常燈
及ヒ厠等ヲ
毀損シ
タル者

（十六）
道路橋梁其他ノ
場所傍ニシタル通
行禁止及ヒ指道標ノ
類ヲ毀棄汚損シタル者

15. Damaging or destroying trees alongside the road, city-owned street lamps or toilets is in violation.

13. It is illegal to build a house, shop or wall outside the bounds of your property. Also, you may not extend your roof with supporting columns.

16. Removing or destroying signs saying, "No passage for..." along roads, bridges or other places is a violation. The same applies for...

...any road signs.

14. Opening a shop stall on the side of the road or by the river without official permission is a violation.

第四百三十八条

左ノ諸件ヲ犯シタル者ハ一日ノ

拘留ニ處シ又ハ八十銭以上

一円以下ノ科料ニ處ス

官署ヨリ價額ヲ定メタル

物品ヲ定價ニ

販賣

（一）

シタル者

（二）

渡船橋梁其他ノ場所ニ

於テ定價以上ノ通行銭ヲ取リ

又ハ故ナク通行ヲ

妨ゲタル者

30

2. If the operators of a bridge, ferry or other crossing charges more than the prescribed fee, it is a violation. This also includes preventing people from crossing for no reason.

Ferry

Article #428

Any person found violating the following rules will be subject to one day in detention in addition to a fine of at least 10 Sen but less than 1 Yen.

1. Selling items above the price prescribed by officials is a violation.

違式詿違条例

5. Setting up a stage and holding performances or setting up an exhibition without a permit is a violation. This also applies to those violating the terms of their permit.

3. Any person who crosses a bridge or takes a ferry without paying the toll is in violation. This applies to any place where there is a fee for crossing.

6. Damaging or altering a drainage ditch, sewer or canal so that water fails to flow properly is a violation. Failure to comply with an order to clean a ... drainage ditch is also a violation.

4. Operating any sort of gambling game on the side of the road is a violation.

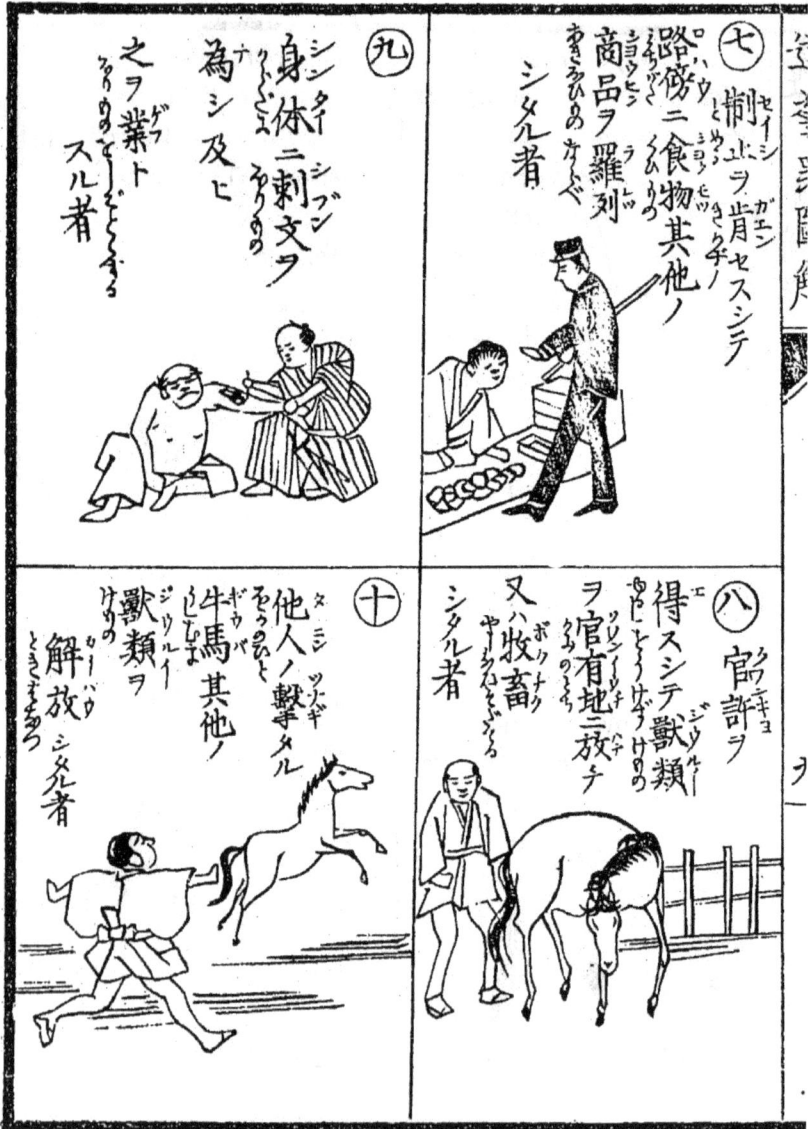

9. Any person getting a tattoo is in violation. This applies to any person applying tattoos as well.

Note: Tattoo is written as 刺文 "stabbed writing" and read as Shibun or Horimono.

7. Failure to comply with an order to stop selling food on the side of the road is a violation. This applies to selling any goods on the side of the road.

10. Untying or otherwise freeing another person's horse or cow is a violation. This applies to any animals being raised by another person.

8. Allowing animals to graze on government property without permission is a violation. This also applies to…

…raising animals on government land.

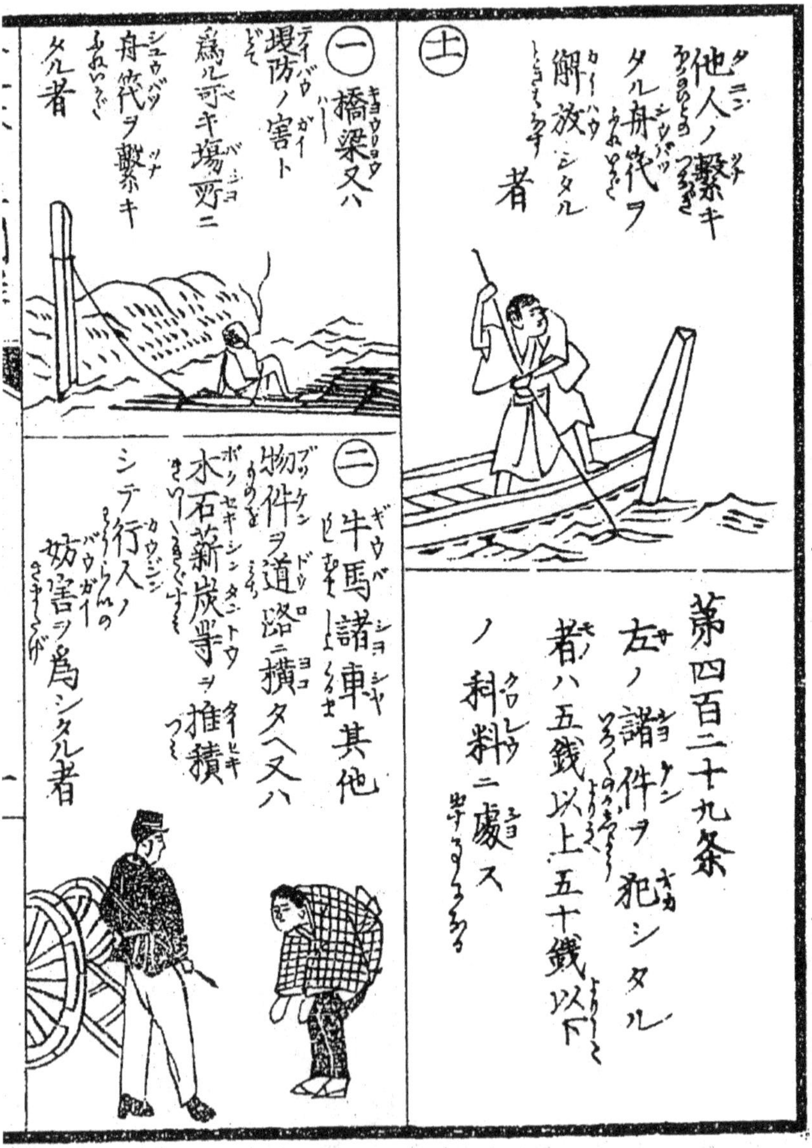

第四百二十九条

左ノ諸件ヲ犯シタル者ハ五銭以上五十銭以下ノ科料ニ處ス

（十一）他人ノ繋キタル舟筏ヲ擅放シタル者

（一）橋梁又ハ堤防ノ害ト爲ル可キ場所ニ舟筏ヲ繋キタル者

（二）牛馬諸車其他物件ヲ道路ニ横タヘ又ハ水石薪炭等ヲ推積シテ行入ノ妨害ヲ爲シタル者

1. Any person tying a boat to a bridge, embankment or any other place that will cause damage is a violation.

2. Blocking the side of a street with a horse, cart or other such vehicle is a violation. This also applies to anyone who blocks the free travel of people with stacks of lumber, stone, kindling, charcoal and so on.

11. Untying another person's boat and using it is a violation.

Article 429

Violators of the following articles will be subject of a fine of greater than 5 Sen but less than 15 Sen.

違式詿違圖解 二

十一

五

氷雪蘆芥
等ヲ道路ニ
投棄シ
タル者

三

車馬ヲ並ヘ
牽テ行人ノ
妨害ヲ為シ
タル者

六

官署ノ
督促ヲ
受ケテ道路ノ
掃除ヲ爲
サザル者

四

水路ニ於テ
船ヲ並ヘ通舩ノ
妨害ヲ爲シタル者

5. Leaving a humongous snowball or pile of rubbish in the middle of the road is a violation.

3. Blocking the road to pedestrians by pulling carts or horses parallel to each other is a violation.

6. Failure to clean the street after an order by an official is a violation.

4. Blocking a canal or waterway by tying boats beside each other is a violation.

（七）
制止ヲ
肯セスシテ路上ニ
旋劇ヲ為シ
行人ノ妨害ヲ
為シタル者

（九）
出入ヲ禁シ
タル場所ニ濫リニ
出入シタル
者

（八）
牛馬ヲ牽
又ハ繋クヲ
怨々ニシテ行人ノ
妨害ヲ
為シタル者

（十）
通行禁止ノ
傍示ヲ犯シテ
通行シタル者

十二

9. Any person entering, for mischievous purposes, an area that has been labeled "no trespassing" is in violation.

7. Ignoring an order to stop doing a performance or play in the street and continuing to block the free movement of pedestrians is a violation.

10. Any person ignoring a "this road or bridge is closed to traffic" sign is in violation.

8. Anyone who impedes pedestrians by leading a horse or a cow is in violation. This also applies to using a long lead rope on an animal.

13. It is a violation to extinguish a streetlight.

11. Any person ignoring an order to stop singing or shouting in a loud voice in the middle of the road is in violation.

14. Any person pasting bills or writing graffiti on the walls of a house is in violation.

12. Drunkards fighting in the street are both in violation. Also anyone lying on the ground incapacitated from drunkenness is in violation.

（十五）
郵宅ノ番号ヲ標ム
招牌又ハ他家ノ貼紙
報告ノ榜標等シ
毀損シタル者

（十七）
公園ノ
規則ヲ
犯シタル
者

（十六）
通路ナキ
他人ノ田圃ヲ
通行シ又ハ
牛馬ヲ牽
ハレタル者

十二

（十八）
他人ノ田野圃圃ニ
菜蔬ヲ
又ハ花卉ヲ
採折シ
タル者

15. Switching the wooden house number plates on the neighborhood signboard is a violation. This also includes damaging paper advertisements of homes for sale or rent or any other such notices.

17. Any person not following the park rules is in violation.
Note: This seems to be regulating taking flowers, fruit or other flora.

18. Any person walking across another person's rice field or garden is in violation. This also applies to those

leading a cow or horse through another person's property.

16. A person taking food from another person's rice field, farm or orchard is in violation. This also applies to collecting flowers.

第四十三条　前数条ニ記載スルノ外各地方ノ便宜ニヨリ定ムル所ノ違警罪ヲ犯シタル者ハ其罪則ニ従テ処断ス

同年同月廿日出版

明治十四年二月七日御願

出版人

編輯人

愛知縣平民　今江五郎
名古屋區住吉町七十番邸

同　寺澤松之助
名古屋區末廣町九十六番邸

Directive 430

In addition, to the many regulations listed on the previous pages, each area has the authority to adjust them as they see fit. It is up to the authorities to judge how the law will be applied to people who break the law.

Published February 7th of Meiji 14 (1881)
Editor : Imae Goro
A "Heimin" Commoner from Aichi Prefecture

Publisher : Terazawa Matsunosuke
A "Heimin" Commoner from Aichi Prefecture